Preface

THIS BOOK is a photographic journey along the River Ribble from its source to the sea. It makes no claim to be a general history of the valley; rather it gives a glimpse into the past of many of the towns and villages found along the river's course.

The illustrations are drawn largely from the library collections in Lancashire and North Yorkshire.

I hope the book will be enjoyed by those who know and love this attractive and varied belt of countryside.

The Ribblehead Viaduct—one of the most remarkable feats of engineering to be found along the Ribble Valley.
(Courtesy of Mr Peter Fox.)

Vanishing Scenes
of the
Ribble Valley

by Jean Harrison

Lancashire County Books
1993

Vanishing Scenes of the Ribble Valley
by Jean Harrison

Published by Lancashire County Books, 143 Corporation Street, Preston

Copyright © Jean Harrison, 1993

Typeset by Carnegie Publishing Ltd., 18 Maynard Street, Preston
Printed by H. Charlesworth & Co., Huddersfield

ISBN 1-871236-24-X

British Library Cataloguing-in-Publication Data
A CIP catalogue record for this book is available from the British Library

Acknowledgements

I WOULD LIKE TO THANK the following people for all the help they have given me in providing photographs and information for this book: the staff of the libraries at Whalley, Clitheroe, Accrington, Haslingden, Preston, Leyland and St Annes; Diana Winterbotham and Zoë Lawson from the Local Studies Library at the Lancashire Library Headquarters; Mr B. J. N. Edwards, County Archaeologist for Lancashire; Kathy Pitt from Skipton Library and Jonathan Blyth from North Yorkshire Library Headquarters; Mr W. R. Mitchell; Mr Peter Fox; Mr W. F. Harrison; Mrs M. Firth and Mr H. Holgate.

Picturesque Horton in Ribblesdale with Penyghent seen in the distance dominating the skyline.
(Courtesy of Skipton Library.)

The Ribble Valley in Yorkshire

THE SOURCE of the River Ribble lies high up in the Yorkshire Dales, where a profusion of streams feed into the Gayle and Cam Becks. It is the confluence of these two becks which marks the point where the Ribble, by name, begins. However, our journey starts at the Ribblehead Viaduct which is, in fact, several miles north of the confluence. The viaduct is one of the most remarkable feats of railway engineering, consisting of twenty-four arches, which span a total of 1,328 feet. It was originally known as 'Batty Moss Viaduct' taking its name from the area upon which it was built. Work began on the viaduct in 1869. Soon a shanty town of around 2000 people was created by the workers and their families between Batty Green and the head of Blea Moor. The work was gruelling and several lives were lost before the viaduct was completed. It was opened on 29 April 1875, when a special train conveyed the Midland Railway Company directors over the whole of the new Settle to Carlisle railway line. In August of that year goods traffic was carried on the line for the first time.

Despite attempts to close the line in recent years, repairs were carried out on the viaduct in 1989 which should ensure its future at least in the short-term. Steam trains still occasionally run on the line as leisure excursions for enthusiasts.

The first village to be reached along the river is picturesque Horton in Ribblesdale, lying at the foot of Penyghent, at an altitude of 770 feet. Its parish church, dedicated to Saint Oswald, dates from Norman times, and was built of local stone from the nearby quarries. Alongside farming, quarrying still provides employment for the villagers.

Stainforth, the next village along the Ribble, is noteworthy for its old packhorse bridge. Before the advent of railways and canals most goods, including heavy loads such as limestone and coal, were carried by packhorse and bridges were in due course built on well-used routes. Packhorse bridges frequently have very low parapets so that the ponies' packs could clear them as the packhorse went across. This bridge was built in the 1670s by Samuel Watson, owner of the nearby Knight Stainforth Hall, and currently belongs to the National Trust. The route is believed to be Roman, running over Malham Moor and into Wharfedale from a camp at Smearsett.

Although predominantly rural, the Langcliffe area in north Ribblesdale had several mills for the manufacture of textiles and paper. Early textile factories were built not in towns, but in the country, on rivers

The seventeenth-century packhorse bridge at Stainforth, thought to be on a much older route of Roman origin.
(From the Bertram Unne Collection, courtesy of the North Yorkshire County Library.)

One of a series of weirs constructed on the Ribble in the Langcliffe area to supply water to the textile and paper mills.
(Courtesy of Skipton Library.)

This unusual well near Giggleswick 'ebbs and flows' like a tide.
(Courtesy of Skipton Library.)

which could power a waterwheel. Paper mills, too, needed large quantities of water for the papermaking process. To supply these mills in Langcliffe a series of weirs was constructed along the Ribble. Working in these mills, set against a background of picturesque limestone hills, was a far cry from toiling in the dirty polluted towns normally associated with the cotton industry, although low wages and poverty would still have existed.

To the west of Langcliffe and a short distance away from the Ribble is an unusual phenomenon, the Ebbing and Flowing Well, near Giggleswick. The water in the well is fed from a source in Giggleswick Scar, eventually entering the Ribble further downstream. The well does not look unusual but at certain times it fills to overflowing and then quickly becomes empty: it 'ebbs and flows' like a tide. This is most noticeable at times of moderate rainfall. In addition a 'silver cord' can sometimes be seen, which is caused by a current of air 'stretching through the water between the two lower outlets'.

On Maundy Thursday crowds of children used to visit the well to make 'spanish juice', by mixing sticks of liquorice with wellwater. This was then stored overnight in the dark to allow the water to absorb the colour and flavour and the following day the children drank it.

The picturesque village of Giggleswick nestling on the edge of the Ribble is best known for its public school. However, Giggleswick achieved national importance for a few seconds on 29 June 1927. The village was chosen by the Astronomer Royal, Sir Frank Dyson, as the most suitable place in the country to view the total eclipse of the sun, the first for 200 years. The eclipse took place at 6.24am and lasted twenty-three seconds, Giggleswick being the only spot where the total phase could be seen uninterrupted.

Thousands of people from all over the country flocked to Giggleswick to view this momentous event. The cinema remained open all night. 'Eclipse Dances' were organised, with dancing until six in the morning, and special services were held in the churches. A road sign was erected by the Automobile Association beside the A65 near Settle to commemorate the event, but it no longer survives.

Settle is the first large town of any importance along the Ribble. It is an old established market town. As early as 1249 Henry Percy, the lord of the manor, was granted permission to hold a market there. The cattle market was of great importance. Beasts could be purchased and then slaughtered in the Shambles, the building with a series of arches facing the market place. Workshops, storerooms and a blacksmith's forge were also incorporated into this block of buildings.

Overlooking Settle is Castleberg, a perpendicular limestone rock about 300 feet high. From its summit on a clear day it is possible to see as far as Pendle in the south

Above: The Automobile Association road sign erected to commemorate the total eclipse of the sun in 1927. (Courtesy of Mr W. R. Mitchell.)
Right: The Market Place, Settle, with the arches of the Shambles behind. The cars in the foreground were assembled for a Motor Meet which took place in Settle in 1904.

Cheapside, Settle, overlooked by the impressive limestone rock of Castleberg.
(Courtesy of Skipton Library.)

Schoolgirls at Rathmell tending their garden plots, c. 1909.
(Courtesy of Mr W. F. Harrison.)

The village green at Long Preston, showing the Holgate Memorial Fountain on the left, and the War Memorial on the right.
(Courtesy of Skipton Library.)

and Penyghent in the north. Situated at the foot of Castleberg is the oldest building in Settle, 'The Folly', built in 1675. It was intended as a residence for the Preston family but owing to lack of funds was never completed: hence the name 'The Folly'.

A few miles downriver from Settle is the village of Rathmell which has one claim to fame. It was the home of the first nonconformist college in England, founded in 1670 by Richard Frankland, a native of the village. Its purpose was to give instruction to candidates for the ministry to whom the universities were then closed. During its chequered history about 300 nonconformist ministers were trained there. The college was later converted into a row of cottages which became known as College Fold. Frankland died in Rathmell in 1698 and was buried in Giggleswick Church.

The village children of Rathmell had received the benefit of education since the early eighteenth century, when George

Clarke bequeathed a piece of land for the purpose of maintaining a schoolmaster there. At this time reading was taught free of charge but instruction in writing and accounts had to be paid for. However, the village school itself was not built until 1845, further rebuilding being carried out in 1875. In the early years of this century Rathmell School took great pride in its garden, each child having a small plot to look after. Prizes were awarded annually to the children with the best-kept gardens.

Long Preston, meaning 'Long Priests Town', is an ancient village and was mentioned in the Domesday Book as 'Pristine'. It has a traditional village green, with a war memorial and a rather impressive fountain given to the village in 1869 by Thomas Holgate of Brooklands in memory of his father. Like many villages along the Ribble, Long Preston developed as a small industrial centre involved in calico manufacture.

The railway bridge over the Keighley to Kendal road in Hellifield, c. 1904.
(Courtesy of Mr W. R. Mitchell.)

A few miles from Long Preston is Hellifield, which grew during the 1870s from a small village into a thriving railway town. Just outside the town is one of the most ancient halls to be seen along the Ribble Valley, Hellifield Peel. This was built during the reign of Henry VI by Lawrence Hammerton. Peel Towers were erected in the north of England as a defence against raids from the Scots which became frequent after the Battle of Bannockburn. Hellifield Peel remained the home of the Hammerton family until 1948, when the house was sold and allowed to fall into ruin. A legend relates that the Hammertons built an underground passage from the Peel to their other home at Wigglesworth Hall; stories of underground passages of this kind are told of many halls, but almost all are fictitious.

Gisburn to Chatburn

JUST SOUTH OF HELLIFIELD the river flows across the boundary between the present counties of Yorkshire and Lancashire. Gisburn is the first settlement of any size on the Lancashire side of the Ribble. This was a busy market town noted particularly for its cattle market; being at a crossroads it was also an important centre for communication. Along the Clitheroe–Skipton turnpike road, through the middle of the town, plied the stage coaches which travelled regularly between Blackburn and Skipton. As yet no trunk road bypasses the town and Gisburn remains a thoroughfare for east–west traffic.

On the opposite side of the river lies the Gisburn Park Estate which covers about 40,000 acres of land centring on the hall built by the Lister family. The first Lord Ribblesdale, Thomas Lister (1752–1820) had a passion for developing his estates in Craven; it was claimed that he could ride from Pendle Hill to Malham Tarn on his own land. Until just over a century ago white cattle grazed in the park. They were said to have been brought to Gisburn from Whalley at the time of the dissolution. Gisburn Park was also the home of a herd of deer, the stags being kept at Deer House Farm, from where they were taken to the hunting grounds.

The quaint village of Bolton by Bowland is unusual in the fact that it has two village greens. The lower one is the site of the old market cross and village stocks. Across the green is Stocks House which

The main street in Gisburn, c. 1930, a thoroughfare for east–west traffic, as it is today.

was built during the early nineteenth century. There was formerly an outside staircase leading to a reading room with a billiard table in the upper storey. The village became a popular spot for day trippers, particularly cyclists, at the turn of the century. The lower storey of Stocks House was then used as a coffee tavern and village shop.

Nearby and overlooking the Ribble Valley was Bolton Hall, the ancestral home of the Pudsay family. It was here that Henry VI went into hiding, following his defeat at the Battle of Hexham. From that time one of the rooms was always referred to as King Henry's Room. Sadly, Bolton Hall was demolished during the 1950s.

A well-known member of the Pudsay family was William Pudsay, who found silver in his lead mines near Rimington and began to mint his own coins known as the Pudsay shillings. Unfortunately he marked them with an escallop, which was the Tower Mint mark of 1584. When one of his

A picturesque view of Rimington village, once the home of the composer Francis Duckworth.

The village of Sawley, showing on the extreme left the two arches astride the road.

employees tried to spend the shillings, word soon leaked out about his illegal activities. Officers were sent to arrest him and he made his escape on horseback, by jumping over Rainsber Scar to the other side of the river. Since then Rainsber Scar has become known as Pudsay's Leap. The traditional story ends with William receiving a pardon from Queen Elizabeth I who was reputed to be his godmother.

A few miles east from Rainsber Scar is the village of Rimington, once the home of Francis Duckworth, a composer of hymn tunes. He is especially remembered for his setting of the hymn 'Jesus shall reign where e'er the sun' to a tune named after the village.

Nearby is a disused lead mine reputed to have produced the silver for Pudsay's mint.

Lying on the banks of the Ribble is the village of Sawley. It has always been predominantly a farming community, although in the late eighteenth century the Peel family established a calico print works there which became a major employer until it closed in 1818.

Sawley originally developed around a Cistercian abbey founded there in 1147, some 150 years before Whalley Abbey. The construction of Whalley Abbey aroused protests from the monks of Sawley, for they considered the new abbey to be a rival and competitor for their alms. By the

Grindleton, one of the highest villages in the Ribble Valley, and home in the seventeenth century of the unorthodox religious sect, the 'Grindletonians'.

time of the dissolution, Sawley had become one of the poorest Cistercian abbeys. Nevertheless, the monks fought hard against the dissolution and the last Abbot, William Trafford, was hanged for his part in the Pilgrimage of Grace in 1536. The abbey ruins may still be seen, though little remains of the original structure, many of the stones being appropriated for use in later village buildings.

At one time Sawley had two arches built of stone from the abbey ruins which stood astride the road in the village. They eventually proved a hazard to traffic, a lorry actually crashing into one, and they were removed into the enclosure of the abbey ruins. Sadly, only one survives today.

The upland village of Grindleton is one of the highest villages in the Ribble Valley and is thought to date back to Saxon times. Until the advent of the powerloom, Grindleton was a centre for handloom weaving. In addition it had a small jam factory and a felt hat works, all long since gone.

Grindleton achieved modest fame in the seventeenth century when an unorthodox religious sect, the 'Grindletonians', took its name from the village. Religious heresy was widespread in these regions at the time and Roger Brearley, the curate of Grindleton Church from 1615 to 1622, founded the sect. He became an important radical preacher and people travelled from miles around to hear him speak. Brearley was greatly persecuted for his teachings and in 1617 was held prisoner at York. The Grindletonians are often seen as a forerunner of the Quaker movement.

Below Grindleton is the ancient village of West Bradford which is believed to date from the reign of Edward II. In the centre of West Bradford is an old cotton mill, a relic of the village's lone encounter with the Industrial Revolution. The building, which originated as a corn

West Bradford with the cotton mill in the background which was owned by the Holgate family for almost a hundred years. (Courtesy of Mr H. Holgate.)

The blacksmith at Waddington, c. 1890. The house still stands today, near the church, and is known as 'Smithy Cottage'.

mill powered by a waterwheel, was later used for several purposes including chair making, bobbin turning and bone crushing, before it was converted to a cotton mill by the Holgate family in 1867. The mill was much extended and employed fifty people working seventy looms at the turn of the century. The Holgates owned the mill until 1960 when it was sold to Trutex of Grindleton. The site is currently being considered for residential development.

A few miles south of West Bradford is the pretty village of Waddington, which has won the award for the best kept village on several occasions. Waddington is thought to mean 'farmstead associated with Wada'. A local story identifies Wada as an Anglo-Saxon chief reported to have camped in Waddington before leading his men into battle against the King of Northumbria at Billangahoth (Langho) in AD 798. The parish church has a stained glass window tracing the history of the

Workmen in Bishop's tile yard, near Waddington, c. 1880.

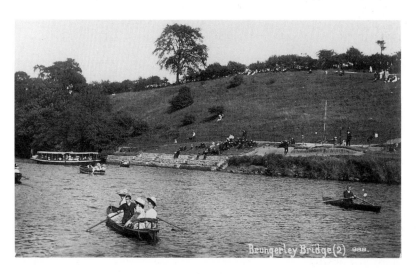

Brungerley Bridge, a popular spot for day-trippers before the First World War.

village which includes a portrait of Wada the Anglo-Saxon chief.

The old village stocks still survive by the church and nearby is 'Smithy Cottage' which as the name suggests was the old blacksmith's house.

Just outside Waddington, on land belonging to Brungerley Farm, there used to be a tile works. It was owned by the Bishop family from the early 1870s until 1950, at which time it was taken over by the Accrington Brick and Tile Company and subsequently ceased operation. The yard made land drainage tiles for agricultural purposes.

Prior to the erection of a bridge over the Ribble at Brungerley it was impossible to reach Clitheroe from Waddington except by means of 'hipping-stones' or stepping stones which could only be crossed safely when the river was low. The wooden bridge which was eventually constructed was washed away in 1814. Shortly afterwards a new stone bridge of three arches was built.

In 1876 Clitheroe Corporation laid out a public park along the riverside at

The headless statue of Peg O'Nell in the gardens of Waddow Hall.

Brungerley. Tea rooms were opened and a small fleet of rowing boats and a motor launch attracted tourists to the area, especially on Bank Holiday Monday. This remained a popular spot until the First World War.

On the banks of the Ribble nearby lies Waddow Hall, which was originally built in Tudor times as a dower house for the Tempest family, who owned the land until 1657. Later the lands came into the possession of the Starkie family, who largely rebuilt the house in Jacobean times. In 1927 Waddow Hall was purchased by the Girl Guides Association and is now an important Commonwealth training centre. It was officially opened by HRH Princess Mary on 1 October of that year.

In front of Waddow Hall is Peg O'Nell's Well and a headless statue. According to legend, Peg O'Nell was a servant girl working for the Starkie family at the hall. Unfortunately she quarrelled frequently with her mistress. One night as Peg grumbled about being sent to fetch some water, Mistress Starkie shouted after her 'I hope you fall and break your neck!' Peg unfortunately did just that. It was said that after that the River Ribble claimed a life every seven years and it became the custom on Peg's Night to drown a dog, cat or a bird to appease Peg's evil spirit. Some time later a statue of Peg was erected at the well where she died.

The story continues that Mistress Starkie had a son who was possessed by a demon. A preacher was sent for to exorcise the spirit but be never arrived. He was found later half-drowned in the river. Mistress Starkie, blaming Peg for what had happened, grabbed an axe, stormed outside and severed the head from the statue. It is said that this put an end to Peg's reign of terror but as a precaution a cock was annually sacrificed in Peg's room for many years to come. Waddow Hall is reputed to be haunted by Peg O'Nell.

Downham, one of the prettiest villages along the Ribble Valley, nestles at the foot of Pendle Hill. As in many villages in the area, the inhabitants combined farming with handloom weaving. A number of the cottages seen in the village today were built for the weavers in the eighteenth century. However, the original settlement is far older than that; it is thought to have existed since Roman times. A Roman road lies to the north of Downham and the remains of two Roman soldiers were uncovered during road improvements in the eighteenth century. They were reburied in the village churchyard.

The Assheton family of Downham Hall has long associations with the village, having virtually owned it for over 400 years. Richard Assheton purchased the hall during the reign of Elizabeth I. The original hall was erected in the 1300s but it has been rebuilt several times since then. The present hall dates from the 1830s, although several parts from the earlier construction

Downham, one of the prettiest villages along the Ribble Valley.

were retained. One member of the Assheton family, Nicholas Assheton, left a remarkable diary which gives a rare insight into early seventeenth-century life in the area. It was published as volume fourteen of the Chetham Society series in 1848.

In the tiny hamlet of Worston on the side of Pendle Hill a tradition was celebrated annually on 9 November: the election of a mock mayor and corporation. The day of the election was one of great amusement, with rival candidates 'formally' addressing the people of the village to gain their votes. The tone of the occasion is revealed in the address of one John Finch, a railway platelayer, who was successfully elected. He proclaimed that he was well-known to all as a man 'accustomed to work on the straightest lines, and shall be no sleeper'. The mayor was given the honorary title of 'sir', the knighthood being conferred by a 'Patent Process' known only to the town clerk. A mayoral gown and feathered cocked hat were also supplied together with a chain and pendant of office which according to one

observer, bore 'a suspicious resemblance to a saucepan lid'. Sadly, the custom was discontinued in 1904.

There is a large bronze ring set in stone in the ground at Worston village, a relic from the days when bull baiting was a common pastime. The wretched animal would be tethered by the horns to the ring, and taunted mercilessly by bulldogs (hence the name); the dogs themselves would suffer as they were repeatedly tossed by the bull's horns. This cruel sport was banned in 1835.

The building of most architectural interest in the village is Worston Old Hall. The present hall was built in 1577 by Richard Greenacre with materials from the original hall, which had fallen into decay and been demolished. The Greenacre family lived there for the next hundred years; the last direct descendant being Frances, who married Nicholas Assheton of diary fame. On the projecting porch of the hall are three stones with large shields which are said to have come from the ruins of either Sawley or Whalley Abbey

following the dissolution. The shield on the left bears a lion rampant, the one on the right the three fishes (the arms of Whalley) and the central one is quarterly France and England. The hall is now converted into a farmhouse.

Chatburn was originally situated on the old Lancashire–Yorkshire boundary, but it now lies firmly within Lancashire. It is thought that its name is derived from St Chad, who was one of the Bishops of Lichfield, Lancashire at that time being part of the Diocese of Lichfield.

Textile manufacture has played an important part in the life of the village, originally in the form of handloom weaving. With the advent of industrialisation, two cotton mills were established in the village, the Chatburn and the Victoria. The Chatburn Mill, founded in 1823, was converted from an old corn mill to a spinning factory. However, it survived less than ten years, closing in 1832. The Victoria Mill was far more successful. This was originally a silk handloom workshop before Robert Hargreaves and William Ingham took it over in 1859 and established a cotton factory there. The mill, after a chequered history, has recently closed. The site is being redeveloped as residential properties.

Above: The bull-ring at Worston, a relic from the village's bull-baiting days.

Right: A Christmas party at Victoria Mill, Chatburn.

Workforce from the Portland Cement Company, near Chatburn.

In the neighbourhood between Chatburn and Clitheroe limestone is plentiful. This had been quarried for hundreds of years, originally for building stone and agricultural uses. In the nineteenth century quarrying in the area became more intensive. The Bold Venture Lime Works, just outside Chatburn, built a gas works which supplied the village until the 1920s.

Cement production commenced in the area in the late nineteenth century and numerous works were established. One of the earliest, founded in the 1880s, was Portland Cement. Later known as Bellman Park, this works operated until after the First World War. Cement production is still a major source of employment in the Clitheroe area, evidenced by the awesome Castle Cement works which dominates the skyline.

Clitheroe to Whalley

THE ANCIENT TOWN of Clitheroe is the second most important town along the Ribble; Preston holding the premier position. Two limestone hills guard the town; upon one lies the parish church of St Mary Magdalene and on the other the ruins of the Norman castle.

Clitheroe's Norman castle, of which little more than the keep remains, is one of the oldest stone structures in Lancashire and has one of the smallest Norman keeps in England. Its site was selected by Roger de Poitou as a centre for controlling the land bestowed upon him by William the Conqueror. Roger de Poitou was First Lord of the Honor of Clitheroe, an area which eventually stretched as far north as Slaidburn, as far south as Bury and covered about 400 square miles. Today the Honor is in the possession of the Assheton family of Downham.

The castle has been used as a home, a business centre for the Honor of Clitheroe, a prison and a place of worship. The Courts Leet, Halmote Court and Courts Baron were also held here. Until 1895 it remained a separate township exempt from the jurisdiction of the borough. In 1920 the Borough of Clitheroe finally purchased the castle.

The Norman castle at Clitheroe, one of Lancashire's oldest stone structures.

A photograph of the Market Place, Clitheroe, taken before the public library was built, showing Bailey's corn millers on the left with the drinking fountain in front. These were both demolished in 1905 to make way for the library.

Clitheroe is an old established market town, a market having been held there every Saturday since Norman times. All the trading was carried out along the main street leading from the castle to the church, with Market Place itself being the centre of activity. At one time four fairs were held in Clitheroe, the earliest dating back to a charter of King John. Livestock was the principal commodity sold, and according to Langshaw, in his book *Clitheroe's thousand years,* for every animal brought to the market and fair a fixed sum had to be paid, the amount having been fixed for centuries. These charges were 4d. for a horse, 3d. for a pig, 2d. for a cow and ½d. for a sheep. The market moved to its present site at the end of the nineteenth century.

The textile industry was once a main employer of the inhabitants of Clitheroe. Most of the factories were established around the mid-nineteenth century; by 1914 there were thirteen mills in the town. The general decline of the cotton industry in the 1920s and 1930s resulted in the closure of many of Clitheroe's mills. Today only one weaving mill survives.

The first spinning mill to be established in the Clitheroe area was just outside the town at Low Moor. At the end of the eighteenth century Low Moor was created as a factory village. In the early years of the Industrial Revolution mills were built on streams, which provided the power to work the machinery, and were frequently established in isolated areas where no previous settlement existed. Factory owners therefore needed to provide housing near the mill to attract a workforce. A mill was established in 1782 at Low Moor. Under the ownership of John Parker, twenty-eight houses were built to accommodate the workers. In 1799 the mill was taken over by Garnett and Horsfall and by 1827 there were 146 cottages in the village. The owners of the mill not only supplied housing for the workforce but shops and other social amenities. By 1873 Low Moor boasted two grocers, a co-op, a boot and shoemaker's and a post office. Social amenities provided were a school, a church, two chapels, and a mechanics' institute and reading room, but no public house; drinking was discouraged by the mill owners. The mill was still in the ownership of the Garnett family when it closed in 1930. The building was demolished in the 1970s and a housing estate built upon the site.

Low Moor post office was established by the 1870s in an old seventeenth-century house close to the entrance to the mill.

Photograph showing the centre of Mitton village c. 1910, with All Hallows Church in the background.

The village of Mitton was originally situated in both Lancashire and Yorkshire; the two hamlets, of Great Mitton in Yorkshire and Little Mitton in Lancashire, being separated by the Ribble, which was the county boundary. All Hallows church, built in the reign of Edward III, is the dominant feature of the village. Within the church is the Shireburn Chapel which contains the impressive monuments to that family whose ancestral home was Stonyhurst. Also of interest in the church is a leper window through which those afflicted with the disease received gifts of food.

Just below Mitton the River Hodder joins the Ribble and about a mile and a half further on, as the Ribble sweeps into a meander, it is joined by the Calder. Standing on the banks of the Calder near its confluence with the Ribble is the village of Whalley. The village dates from Saxon times and may be on a Roman site, possibly a minor one connected with the Roman fort at Ribchester.

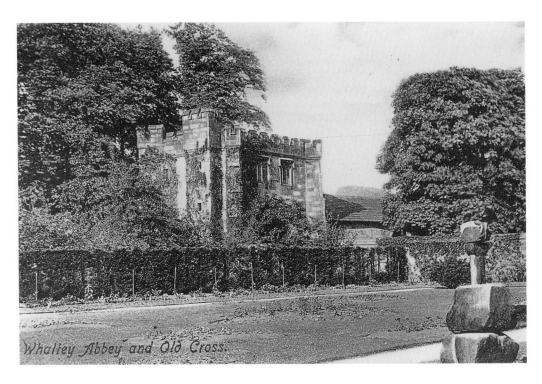

Whalley Abbey and Old Cross.

The castellated north-east gateway to Whalley Abbey built in the fifteenth century.

Whalley is most famous for its abbey ruins. In 1296 the Abbey of Stanlow in north Cheshire was moved to Whalley, the monks having been driven out of Stanlow by repeated flooding. Building on the new site at Whalley then began. The abbey church, built between 1330 and about 1345 was quite large, 110 yards long, 70 yards wide with a 180-foot tower. The last Abbot of Whalley, Abbot Paslew, was involved in the uprising against Henry VIII, known as the 'Pilgrimage of Grace'. Along with some of the monks from Whalley he was eventually tried and executed for his part in the affair. The abbey was subsequently seized by the king and after its dissolution the property passed into the hands of the Assheton family of Downham Hall. Richard Assheton converted the abbot's lodgings into an Elizabethan manor house. It remained a private residence until 1923 when the whole property was acquired by the Church of England.

The parish church in Whalley is well worth a visit. It was established long before the abbey was built; the Domesday Book refers to the Church of St Mary in Whalley. However, the present building dates from about 1200. Inside the church are choirstalls dating from the fifteenth century which previously belonged to the abbey. In the churchyard are three stone crosses dating back probably to the tenth and eleventh centuries.

The village of Whalley has retained a traditional charm with its old farm workers' cottages and well-preserved Georgian houses which line the main street. Four inns cluster around the centre, three of which, the Dog, the Swan and the Whalley Arms (now called the Hog's Head) date from the eighteenth century. The village was a resting place for the mail coaches travelling to Manchester at that time, the Swan being the coaching inn. The Whalley Arms was built with stone from the ruined

The main street in Whalley showing the Whalley Arms on the left and the Nab rising in the distance.

Whalley Post Office staff in 1902. The postmaster, Mr Camm, is third on the left.

Portfield Hall, some of which had been appropriated from the abbey. In the 1860s the fourth inn, the De Lacy Arms, was built on the site of the ancient manor house of Whalley.

Spanning the skyline above Whalley is the viaduct which was built in the late 1840s as a railway bridge across the River Calder. It is 2037 feet long and has 49 arches. With the reopening of the line from Clitheroe to Blackburn in recent years, trains now pass over the viaduct again and steam trains can be seen on special excursions in the summer months.

Stonyhurst to Walton-le-Dale

STONYHURST COLLEGE dominates the Ribble Valley at this point and is its most majestic building. For more than four centuries it was the ancestral home of the Shireburn family. The building was started by Hugh Shireburn as early as 1523. The most notable member of that family was Sir Richard Shireburn who lived at Stonyhurst for fifty-seven years. He was Master Forester of the Forest of Bowland, Steward of the Manor of Slaidburn, Lieutenant of the Isle of Man and Deputy Lieutenant of Lancashire. The last of the Shireburns to live at Stonyhurst was Sir Nicholas, whose son died at the age of eight after eating some poisonous berries. The family then became extinct in the male line. After passing to the Weld family, the property was eventually given to the English Jesuit foundation in Liege, Belgium.

The establishment of the college at Stonyhurst dates from 1794 when a party of Jesuits arrived, having fled from a revolution in Belgium. It is now one of the most famous Roman Catholic public schools in the country. It possesses a large library containing many rare works, including a collection of beautifully illuminated ancient missals, a copy of St Cuthbert's Gospel and volumes by early printers such as Caxton. In the college museum are preserved examples of ancient ecclesiastical vestments and other notable items such as Saint Thomas More's cap, and a jewelled prayer book of Mary Queen of Scots. Within the grounds is the magnificent church of St Peter built by the Jesuits in 1835 following the 1829 Catholic Emancipation Act which eased restrictions on the building of Catholic churches.

The village of Hurst Green lies in the shadow of Stonyhurst and has been traditionally associated with the Shireburn family. Close to Stonyhurst are the almshouses built by Nicholas Shireburn in 1706. These were originally situated at Kemple End on Longridge Fell but were

The military band of Stonyhurst taken outside the college in 1913. St Peter's Church can be seen on the right.

Almshouses built by Nicholas Shireburn in 1706. Originally situated at Kemple End, they were removed to Hurst Green in 1946.

ALMS HOUSES, KEMPLE END, BUCK, PHOTO.

Ferry boat crossing the river from Dinckley Hall in 1927.

removed to their present position in Hurst Green in 1946. The Shireburn Arms is a further indication of the family's presence in the village.

Another public house in Hurst Green, the Punchbowl, is reputed to be haunted by the highwayman Ned King who used the inn as a hiding place. He was captured and supposedly hanged from a nearby tree.

A short distance from Hurst Green is Dinckley Ferry. Before a footbridge was

built across the Ribble in 1951 a ferry operated here, originally to connect Dinckley Hall with the main routes in the county. The first ferry was a 'trowsferry' which consisted of two hollowed out logs which were pulled backwards and forwards by ropes across the river. This was later replaced by a rowing boat.

Dinckley Hall, a partly timber-framed Tudor building, is now used as a farm-house. In the past it has been the home of

Excavating the Roman fort at Ribchester in 1914. The headquarters of the fort was found on the site photographed here. The parish hall was subsequently built upon it.

The White Bull Hotel, Ribchester, with its four columns holding up the portico which are believed to have supported a Roman temple.

several notable families including the de Clitheroe family, the Talbots and Lord de Tabley. It is currently owned by the Duke of Somerset and farmed by a tenant.

Ribchester with its Roman remains is one of the most famous villages along the Ribble. There is evidence to show that a settlement existed near here long before the Romans came, as burial urns have been found from the Bronze Age. The permanent Roman fort, Bremetennacum, dates from about AD 79. It was built to accommodate a cavalry troop of around 500 men and horses. The original fort covered an area of just under 6 acres and housed a cavalry unit. The Roman garrison left Ribchester at the end of the fourth century AD.

In 1883 excavations began and one of the principal features to be discovered was part of the Roman granaries, followed later by the discovery of the bath house. One of the most spectacular discoveries in the area was a Roman hoard found by a young boy in 1796. The hoard included a bronze ceremonial helmet ornamented with armed soldiers in fighting attitudes. The original is housed in the British Museum, while a replica is on display in the museum at Ribchester.

Ribchester itself is rather quaint with its long rows of stone terraced cottages, some of which were originally built for handloom weavers. This was the main occupation of the villagers until two

Stydd almshouses built by John Shireburn of Stonyhurst in 1726.

weaving mills were established in the nineteenth century. Ribchester at this time was a thriving industrial community with a variety of shops to support it. Only one mill survives today and the village is now largely a residential and tourist centre. In addition to the Roman remains and museum, the village also has a Museum of Childhood.

Of architectural note is the White Bull Hotel. The four columns holding up the portico at the front are believed to have once supported a Roman temple. Also of interest are the old almshouses at Stydd which were built by John Shireburn in 1726 to accommodate 'five old and infirm women professing the Catholic faith'. They are still inhabited, but have been modernised. Nearby stands Stydd Church, one of the oldest places of worship in the Ribble Valley. The original chapel was built by the Knights Hospitallers of St John of Jerusalem in the late twelfth century.

A few miles west of Ribchester, set among the fells at the edge of the Forest of Bowland, is the small town of Longridge. Although the settlement dates from the fifteenth century it was the Industrial

Revolution which provided the impetus for its development. Stone which had been quarried on a small scale for local use now became an important building material for the ever growing industrial towns, and quarries were opened at Tootle Height and Chapel Hill to satisfy this demand. In 1840 a railway was built to transport the stone to Preston. Several impressive buildings in Preston are built with Longridge stone, including the Harris Library, Museum and Art Gallery and Fulwood Barracks. The railway also enabled the transportation of cotton, which led to the establishment of four mills near the line in the mid-nineteenth century. Longridge had previously possessed a handloom weaving community. Today quarries, mills and railways are all long since gone.

Up on the fells outside Longridge stands Written Stone Farm in which lies a large rectangular stone some 9 feet long and 2 feet wide inscribed with the words 'Rauffe Radcliffe laide this stone to lye forever. A.D. 1655'. Rauffe Radcliffe was the owner of the estate at this time and chose this unusual way to perpetuate his name. It is said that at one

Workman from Longridge Quarry Company at Tootle Heights, c. 1900.

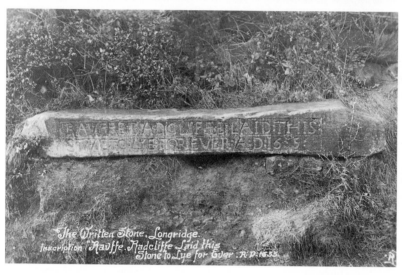

Rauff Radcliffe chose an unusual way to perpetuate his name in the written stone which stands outside a farm on Longridge fells.

time the stone was moved by former occupants of the farm to make a buttery stone, but whenever pots, pans or crockery were placed on it they overturned. They were even heard to clatter during the night. The stone was then returned to its original site and peace was restored.

On the south bank of the Ribble a few miles west of Longridge lies Samlesbury. This village had one brief claim to fame when it became involved in the Lancashire witch trials of 1612. Three Samlesbury

women, Jennet and Ellen Brierley and Jane Southworth, were accused of witchcraft but were later acquitted.

The village church is well worth a visit for it contains some beautifully carved old pews dating from the seventeenth century and a double-decker pulpit. In the churchyard there is a broken gravestone held down by iron spikes. Folklore says that these spikes were used to prevent uneasy spirits from leaving their graves. However, a more likely explanation is that the spikes

Left: Samlesbury Hall, one of the most impressive buildings in the Ribble Valley with its striking Tudor style black and white façade.

Below: The unveiling of the stone which marks the site of the Cuerdale Hoard, by Mr Ralph Assheton (who later became Lord Clitheroe) on 3 October 1948. To his right are his wife, Alderman W. Gordon and Mr Frank Coupe, the last being responsible for organising the scheme.

were placed there to deter body-snatchers, who would unearth newly laid bodies and sell them to doctors for dissection.

One of the most impressive buildings nearby must undoubtedly be Samlesbury Hall. There has been a hall on the site since at least the late thirteenth century, passing into the possession of the Southworth family during the following century and it was that family who were largely responsible for creating the hall as we know it today. As the Southworths were staunch Catholics and refused to give up the old faith, they had many secret rooms and priest holes built into the house during Elizabethan times in order to hide and avoid persecution. Owing to a loss of prosperity the Southworths were forced to sell the hall to the Bradylls in 1679. The Bradylls, however, never took up residence at Samlesbury and so for a time the hall was used as a tenement for handloom weavers and then became a beerhouse, known as the Bradyll Arms. Later part of the hall was used as a girls' boarding school but in 1862 Joseph Harrison, a wealthy ironfounder from Blackburn, purchased the hall and spent large sums of money restoring it to something of its former glory. The Harrisons having left in 1909, the building more or less fell into ruin until 1924, when a campaign was successfully mounted to save it.

The Cuerdale Hoard, one of the greatest collections of Viking silver, was discovered a few miles downriver from Samlesbury by workmen repairing the Ribble bank in 1840. Some of the coins, thought to have been hidden about the year AD 903, may be seen in the Harris Museum

The Unicorn Inn, Walton-le-Dale, c. 1904. Oliver Cromwell is thought to have slept there after the Battle of Preston in 1648.

and Art Gallery. The rest of the hoard was divided up between various museums and individuals. The site of the find is marked by a stone erected in 1948. An interesting myth recorded before the discovery of the hoard claimed that anyone standing in St Leonard's Church, Walton-le-Dale, and looking upstream was looking over the greatest treasure in Christendom. How true this proved to be.

Walton-le-Dale stands at the confluence of the rivers Darwen and Ribble, just east of Preston. The village is of ancient origin, dating back to Roman times and possibly beyond. It lies close to the Roman road between Chester and Carlisle and is thought to have been an industrial depot for the Roman army, supplying garrisons in the north west.

One of the oldest buildings in Walton-le-Dale today is the Unicorn Inn which dates back to the early seventeenth century. It is associated with Oliver Cromwell who is said to have used the inn as his headquarters during the Battle of Preston in 1648. During Jacobite times the inn became the meeting place for a club known as the 'Mock Corporation of Walton' which in reality was a political club supporting the cause of the Stuarts. By the First World War the inn had been converted into a well-appointed tea-room catering for cyclists and other tourists. It is now Pinocchio's Restaurant.

Preston

SITUATED ON THE NORTH BANK of the Ribble, Preston is the largest town between Ribblehead and the estuary. It is an old established market town; the market dates from the fourteenth century. Prior to the nineteenth century all manner of goods were sold, each type of product having its own allotted position in the market place. Butter, cheese and poultry were on Cheapside, corn, barley and beans on the west side of the square, brass, pewter and hardware in the centre and cloth and hosiery on the east. The cattle and horse markets were on Church Street and Friargate respectively. At eight o'clock a bell would sound and all the townspeople were allowed exclusive access to the stall until nine o'clock, when the stalls were open to people from outside the town and wholesalers. During the nineteenth century some of the market stalls were moved when the covered market and the Corn Exchange were built.

During the Industrial Revolution, Preston developed into an important cotton manufacturing town involved in both spinning and weaving. Among the principal mill owners in the town was the Horrocks family. In 1791, at the age of twenty-three, John Horrocks of Edgeworth founded a business in Preston operating from Turk's Head Yard as a putter out of yarns to handloom weavers. The following year he

Preston Market Place c. 1890, taken from the south side looking towards Friargate.

Weavers at Horrocks' Mill, Preston, c. 1900.

erected his well-known Yard Factory, the original power used being a horse which pulled round a driving shaft – a one-horse-powered cotton mill. During the next ten years he had established seven mills in Preston. As with many successful industrialists of the time, John Horrocks became influential in town affairs and in 1802 became MP for Preston. Two years later he died in London at the early age of thirty-six and he was buried in Penwortham Church. His mills, having passed down through successive generations, survive today and have a worldwide reputation for quality.

For centuries small craft had been able to navigate the Ribble estuary as far as Preston but it was not until the nineteenth century that work began on making the river navigable for larger craft. As early as 1806 the first company was formed by an Act of Parliament to try to clear the silt from the river. This was not very successful, although in 1829 a steamboat became the first vessel of its class to reach Preston. In 1838 Preston merchants joined with this company to form the second Ribble Navigation Company. In 1843 a new quay was constructed opposite the marsh and Preston became an independent port.

Preston Corporation took over the venture in 1883 making it one of the very few municipal ports in the country. It soon became clear that Preston needed a wet dock if the port was to flourish. After great controversy over its construction, which involved diverting the river about a mile, the Albert Dock was opened in 1892. This made Preston one of the most important ports, for the Albert Dock was the largest single dock in the country at that time. Trade greatly increased over the years and goods imported included wood, coal, petroleum and bananas. Preston pioneered the container roll-on roll-off system. However, trade declined severely in the late 1970s and the port closed in 1981. The area has now been dramatically redeveloped as a retail and residential site.

One of Preston's most impressive parks is Avenham Park which lies on the bank of

Preston was once an important port, the Albert Dock built in 1892 being the largest single dock in the country at that time.

the Ribble. The site was laid out in the 1860s by the corporation, who transformed the former orchards and gardens into a natural amphitheatre with pleasant

The Old Tram Bridge in Avenham Park, Preston. The tramway linked the Lancaster with the Leeds and Liverpool Canal and was used for the transportation of coal.

tree-lined walks and formal gardens. The general aim was to provide open space for the health and amusement of the working people, in an attempt to draw them away from the public houses. Drunkenness was considered to be a real problem at the time. The gardens were also to be educational, the various plants being labelled with their botanical names and other relevant information. Later a bandstand was built and open-air musical performances were held regularly in the summer.

On the eastern side of the park was the Old Tram Bridge which was a wooden structure built in 1802. It formed part of a tramway linking the Lancaster Canal with the Leeds and Liverpool Canal and it was used mainly for the transportation of coal. Horse-drawn trains, consisting of eight or nine waggons, traversed the route to Walton Summit, until the tramway closed in 1859. Ownership of the bridge was subsequently transferred to Preston Corporation who transformed it into a public walkway across the river.

South of the Estuary

PENWORTHAM has been a crossing place of the Ribble from early times. Originally ferries plied the river there. Dr Kuerden writing in the seventeenth century refers to a ferry 'where diverse boats are ready as occasion may require for horse or foot to waft them over to the other side'. In 1755 a bridge was built, paid for by public subscription. However it collapsed a year later when one of the central piers gave way. Another bridge was erected in 1759. This was supplemented in 1915 with a much wider one to cope with the heavier traffic. A further bridge has since been built to cater for the ever increasing traffic congestion.

Penwortham village is now almost exclusively a residential area, a suburb of Preston, yet it has had a long and interesting past. On the hill overlooking the Ribble once stood a Norman castle guarding the estuary. The site may still be discerned as a mound to the north of St Mary's Church.

The church is of ancient origin and the site predates the building of the castle. Parts of the present building date from the fourteenth century, though much of the church was rebuilt in the last century. Near the church once stood a medieval priory. The original priory at Penwortham was founded early in the twelfth century. It was connected with Evesham Abbey in Worcestershire. Once a year on the feast of St Egwin the monks of Penwortham had to send sixty salmon, in part payment for the facilities at the priory, to the Abbot of Evesham. At that time salmon were quite abundant in the Ribble. Following the dissolution the Fleetwood family took possession of the priory and built a manor house on the site. They resided there until 1749. In 1783 the Rawstorne family acquired the priory and substantially

Ferry boat over the River Ribble at Penwortham, and in the distance the old Penwortham Bridge, built in 1759.

Penwortham Priory—the manor house built on the site of the medieval priory by the Fleetwood family after the dissolution. It was subsequently rebuilt in this gothic style by the Rawstorne family in the early nineteenth century, only to be demolished in the 1920s.

The old clay pits at Longton, a relic of the brick works founded there at the end of the nineteenth century. The factory only closed in the 1960s and the site has since been redeveloped as a housing estate, though a portion has been retained as a nature reserve.

rebuilt the house in the gothic style. It was in their possession until it was demolished in the 1920s.

The south bank of the estuary from Penwortham to Southport is a vast expanse of marshland. Villages straggle along its edge: Hutton, Longton, Hesketh Bank and Tarleton. Agriculture was the mainstay of life in these parts and to a large extent still is. Much of the agricultural land drained from the marshes in the early nineteenth century is now good fertile soil excellent for arable crops. Today market gardens and nurseries abound.

Longton is mainly a residential village but in the nineteenth century it was not only a thriving farming community but also had a successful brewing industry. There were in fact two breweries at this time, both on Marsh Lane, one owned by James Pye and the other by William and Richard Wilkins. The Wilkins brewery was the larger of the two and the malthouse building survived until 1976, when it was demolished and replaced by a housing estate. In addition, Longton was involved in brick and tile making. Thomas Ward and Company established a firm there in 1897.

The swing bridge over the River Douglas built when the West Lancashire Railway was constructed in 1882 to allow tall vessels to pass through.

Clay was extracted and carried by tramway to brick kilns near the station. The factory closed in the 1960s when the clay was depleted.

Hesketh Bank lies on the west bank of the River Douglas and to the south is the Ribble estuary. It was originally a fishing village with many of its inhabitants earning a living from the river and the sea, some as fishermen, others as mariners carrying cargo along the coast and over to Ireland. An Act of Parliament was passed in 1720 to allow the River Douglas, also known here as the Asland, to be made navigable between Wigan and the Ribble estuary. Later the Douglas Navigation was linked with the Leeds and Liverpool Canal. Vessels plied along this navigation taking coal from Wigan to Preston and Lytham and even to Ireland, and grain, meal and butter were imported. In 1882, when the West Lancashire Railway was constructed, a swing bridge was built over the River Douglas to allow tall vessels to pass.

After the draining of the marsh, farming became the main occupation of villagers around Hesketh Bank and Tarleton. During the first two decades of this century a local photographer, Mr Tatham, recorded life on the farms in the area. Two of his photographs reproduced here show haymaking and strawberry picking.

Southport is on the furthest point of the south bank of the Ribble estuary. It is here where the river meets the sea. Southport is a sedate seaside resort catering essentially for the more refined holidaymaker. This is epitomised by Lord Street, the main thoroughfare of the town, with its wide boulevard lined with elegant shops. The resort was the creation of the two main landowners of the town in the nineteenth century, Charles Hesketh and Charles Scarisbrick, who carefully planned its development to attract the middle-class visitor. Not for Southport the working-class day trippers and charabancs.

Haymaking at Douglas Bank farm, Tarleton, c. 1908.

Strawberry picking at Tarleton in the early years of this century.

Southport pier, opened in 1860, was the first to be built in a Lancashire resort.

The marine lake and gardens, c. 1900, still one of Southport's main attractions.

Nevertheless, Southport did establish the usual seaside entertainments. It was the first of the Lancashire seaside resorts to build a pier; its official opening was in 1860, some three years before Blackpool pier was erected. However, there was serious criticism concerning the length of the walk to the end, the pier being 1200 yards long. In 1863 a tramway was constructed to convey passengers to the end of the pier.

The main attractions of Southport are its marine lake and gardens. Originally there were two lakes, one north and one south of the pier, which were joined in 1895. Nearby a fairground developed which boasted a 'Captive Flying Machine', river caves, helter-skelter and water chute in the early years of this century. In 1922 this fairground was moved to the Pleasureland site, leaving the promenade and pier for more peaceful pursuits.

Southport is perhaps most famous today for its flower show which has a national reputation second only to Chelsea. The first show was held in 1924 and since then thousands of people have flocked to Southport every year to admire the colour and magnificence of the horticultural displays.

North of the Estuary

SITUATED NORTH OF THE ESTUARY at the confluence of the Dow, the Douglas and the Ribble, Freckleton was used as a port from early times. The Romans may have used it to serve the fort at Kirkham. Later, cargoes of wood, slate and grain were transported from Cheshire and shipped up the Douglas to Freckleton. Coal was also carried by barge from Wigan. Freckleton acted as a distribution centre for coal for the Fylde. The coal was unloaded below the Ship Inn near the aptly named Bunker Street. The Ship Inn was reputed to be connected with smugglers, as illegal goods were brought up the river as far as Freckleton and unloaded there.

A shipyard was established near the port in 1814 where schooners, boats and barges were built. Later the yard serviced lifeboats from all over the North of England. The village was also involved in sailcloth manufacture, and in 1880 the Balderston cotton mill was established there. This operated for a hundred years, only closing in 1980. It has since been demolished.

A few miles west of Freckleton lies the village of Warton which is now largely known as one of the main sites for British Aerospace. Until the nineteenth century, however, Warton was an important crossing point of the Ribble, for there used to be a ford across the river between

The Ship Inn and the aptly named Bunker Street at Freckleton, where coal was unloaded for distribution throughout the Fylde. In the foreground is the River Dow.

The Guides House at Warton, a popular tourist haunt in the early part of this century, especially with ramblers and cyclists.

Warton and Hesketh Bank. It was used both by local and long-distance traffic, and a guide was available to lead people over the water. In 1655 William Tomlinson of Warton, the guide over the river, petitioned the sessions of the peace at Preston, saying that during the past forty years he had lost more than ten horses in this service and he asked for an allowance towards the purchase of a new horse.

The ford fell into disuse in the nineteenth century, doubtless affected by the deeper water of the improved navigation channel to Preston. Since then all road traffic between south-west Lancashire and the Fylde has had to make the inconvenient journey upstream to Preston in order to cross the river; a scheme undertaken in 1899 to build a tramroad across the estuary from Southport to Lytham was abandoned ten years later.

The Guides House at Warton was a popular tourist haunt in the early part of this century catering particularly for ramblers and cyclists. The name suggests that this hotel was associated with the guide across the ford. However, the building is a replacement for a much older ale house of the same name. Yates's map of 1786 shows

two 'Guides Houses' at Warton, one of which was probably the inn, and the name must have become attached to any house in which the guide at the time lived. The Guides House was demolished during the Second World War to make way for larger runways for the RAF aeroplanes operating at the airfield nearby.

Windmills were once a familiar sight in the Fylde landscape. Warton used to have a peg mill. This was a wooden structure, three storeys high, with a central post or 'peg', which was about twenty feet long, on which a circular floor turned. The mill was constructed so that it could be turned round bodily according to the wind direction. The peg mill at Warton originally stood at Rufford and was taken across the river ford and reassembled in 1717. A remnant of the wooden structure and a mill stone are all that remain.

In 1847 a lighthouse was built in the approach to the Ribble three miles below Lytham. Prior to this date ships requiring a light to guide them had to fire a gun at sunset. At this signal, a light hung on a pole on Lytham beach would be lit. The new lighthouse was strongly built, but in spite of this it fell down in January 1863, undermined by the action of the sea which

Above: Warton had a different kind of windmill from those usually seen in the Fylde; known as a 'peg' mill, because of the way it was constructed with a central post or 'peg'.
Right: An illustration of the first lighthouse to be built in the Ribble estuary in 1847.

had gradually washed away part of the neighbouring beach on this ever-changing coastline. A new lighthouse, built further inland, was used from 1865 until 1890.

The twin seaside resorts of Lytham and St Annes are at the western point of the northern bank of the Ribble estuary opposite Southport. Like Southport they have an air of grandeur and elegance which has been carefully cultivated.

Lytham was originally a small fishing port and became a resort in response to the sea-bathing craze of the early nineteenth century. As in Southport, the main landowners of the town, the Cliftons, closely supervised the development of the resort and endeavoured to attract the

middle-class tourist while aiming to please the town's residents. The Market Square which was developed by the Cliftons in the mid-nineteenth century presents a good example of this. It is bordered by elegant shops and at its centre is the impressive Market House, built at a cost of £1000 in 1848. A tower and lantern were added to the building in 1872 to house the clock which was a donation from Lady Eleanor Clifton.

Lytham established the usual tourist attractions of a pier (opened in 1865) and promenade, but never had the bawdy entertainments or pleasure beach amusements of its neighbour Blackpool. Lytham was a resort for sedate promenading.

The Market Square, Lytham, taken at the turn of the century, with its elegant shops and at its centre the impressive Market House built in 1848.

Lytham green and its well-known landmark the windmill. Next to the windmill is the old lifeboat house, built largely of cobblestones; another gift from the Clifton family to the people of Lytham.

The green at Lytham, with its well-known landmark the windmill, was a gift of the Clifton family in 1923 which benefited both residents and tourists. It was, and still is today, a place for picnicking and ball games. The windmill was erected in 1805 on what was then Lytham Marsh and was in operation until 1918 when it was damaged by fire. The windmill was restored and is now a tourist attraction in its own right.

In contrast to Lytham, St Annes grew up almost overnight. In fact the idea to build a fashionable resort on the Fylde coast was the brainchild of the Rossendale cotton manufacturer, Elijah Hargreaves. While on holiday in Blackpool he walked along the deserted beach towards Lytham

St Annes pier, c. 1915, showing the Moorish pavilion and the Floral Hall.

and began to visualise an elegant town rising from the sand dunes. On returning to Rossendale, Hargreaves was able to persuade several colleagues to go along with this venture and in 1874 he and seven fellow directors registered the St Annes Land and Building Company. Within the next few years £70,000 was spent on a square mile of land that was to grow into the new resort. The first building to be constructed was the St Annes Hotel in 1875.

During the next decade many impressive buildings sprang up in the town, and one, which perhaps more than any other, helped to reflect the prosperity and success of the venture was the pier. Officially opened in 1885 by Lord Derby, the original pier was 315 yards long. It included a Moorish pavilion with domes which were decorated in gold leaf, and a Floral Hall in which vaudeville artists and orchestras performed to entertain the tourists.

Like Lytham, St Annes aimed to attract the middle-class tourist and its promenade with its bandstand, gardens and paddling pool promoted the image of gentility.

Conclusion

THE RIVER RIBBLE has at last reached the end of its journey from the Pennines to the sea. It has passed through quiet villages and busy market towns, watered the banks of ancestral estates and lapped the skirts of a Roman fort, as it continued on its way to join the Irish Sea.

Here, where the holiday resorts of Lytham and St Annes line the northern shore of the broad estuary we, too, have reached the end of our journey, having seen the region as our parents and grandparents saw it. Happily, time has not removed the charm and interest of this delightful river valley.